Roller-coaster Ride
AROUND THE BODY

WRITTEN BY
GABBY DAWNAY

ILLUSTRATED BY
ALEX BARROW

W
FRANKLIN WATTS
LONDON · SYDNEY

♥ CONTENTS

Dr Ino →

Are you ready to go?
But at first shall we see,
All the things that make YOU
And the things that
make ME?

Ted has red hair, Zack has black, Flo has brown eyes, so does Jack.

 Flo is funny, Ted is tall.

Jack can skip and kick a ball!

 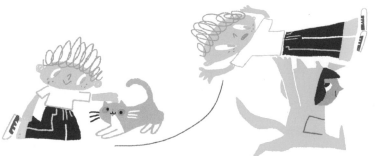

Zack is great at making stuff,

Ted is gentle, Jack is tough!

Flo is fast and Zack can hop, Ted can dance and Jack can't stop...

Zack is dreamy, Jack has jokes:
Different skills for different folks!

Whatever colour, shape or name,
We are different AND the same!

My body, your body, everybody shout:

We all have a body and it's how we move about!

We all have a heart that pumps like a beat,

To the rhythm of life from our head to our feet.

We hear with our ears and see with our eyes,

We think with our brain – that's no surprise!

To keep us warm we have our hair,

We need our lungs to breathe the air.

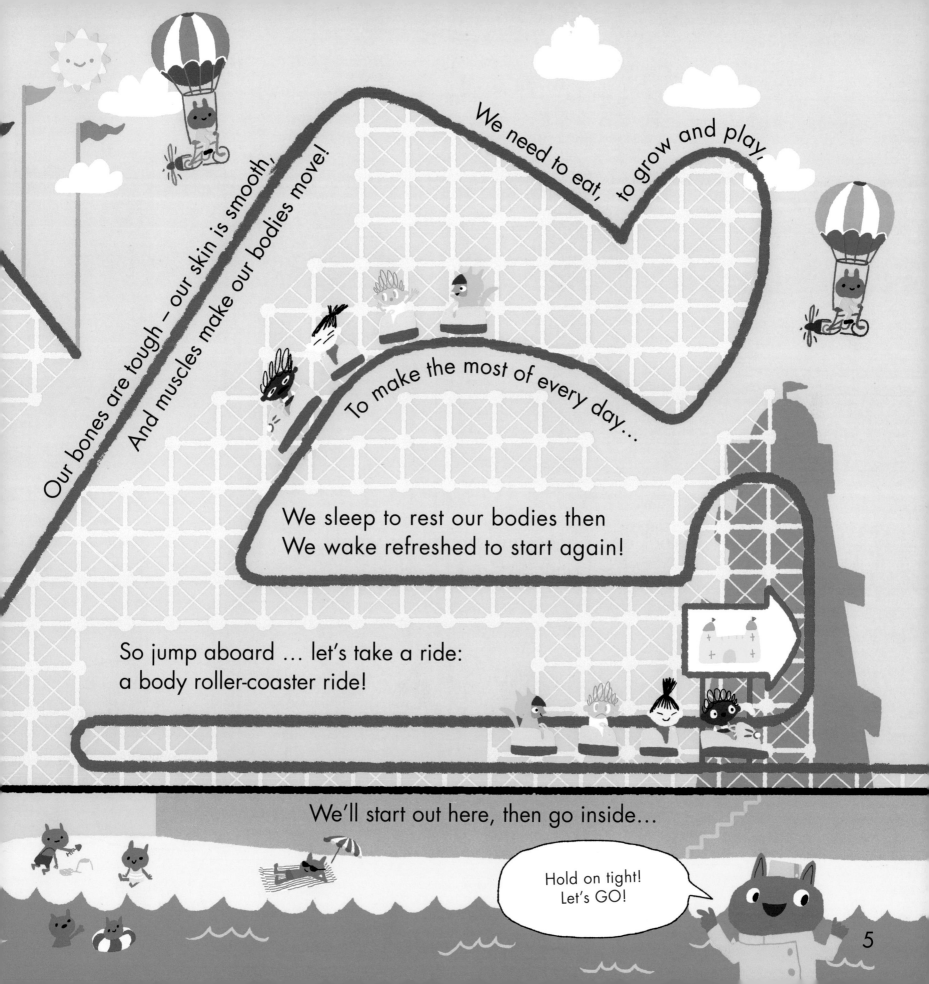

Our bones are tough – our skin is smooth,
And muscles make our bodies move!

We need to eat, to grow and play,

To make the most of every day...

We sleep to rest our bodies then
We wake refreshed to start again!

So jump aboard ... let's take a ride:
a body roller-coaster ride!

We'll start out here, then go inside...

Hold on tight!
Let's GO!

5

Inside out and outside in, why don't we just begin with … SKIN!

Skin's fantastic – it's elastic, skin is also very thin.

Skin keeps all the outside out
And skin holds all your insides … in!

Freckled, tanned and smooth or wrinkly,
After bathing skin is … crinkly!

Waterproof, with weeny hairs,
Skin is tough, though sometimes tears
(But notice how your skin repairs!)

Skin is the body's biggest organ, and through it we can touch the world around us – and keep our squashy insides safe.

DYNAMITE HAIR CUTS

Thick or wispy, short or long,

Plaited, matted, knotted, strong...

Smooth and straight or fun and frizzy,
Mousey, ginger, brown or busy.

Head as shiny as a ball,
when there is
no hair at all.

As well as the hair on our heads, our skin is covered in millions of tiny hairs to keep us warm.

Silver, blonde or black or white. *Any* hair is dynamite!

We're at the fair and here to stay...
Look over there – come on, let's play!

Hop and skip, throw and jump ... can you see my muscles pump?

Touch your toes then stretch up tall, make a face or kick a ball!

Dance and slide,
then shout and sing –
Everybody, do your thing!

8

Play catch, tap and bend, clap your hands with a friend.

Spin, rock, roll and run – laugh aloud and have some fun!

Ride a horse or walk the dog, balance on a wobbly frog!

Muscles move all the different parts of your body. Can you do the actions as you read the words?

Twist and flex and find your groove,
Muscles make your body move!

9

All that playing
sure was great...

I spy food – please pass the plate!

Bite, taste, chew, munch...
This is how I eat my lunch.

Squishing-squashing food to pulp...
Time to swallow with a 'gulp!'

In my tummy ... never resting
Juices start to get DIGESTING.

Swishy-swoshy, do you know
Where the food I eat will go?

Doing even more digesting
Passing through the large intestine.

Now the food you cannot see
Will transform to E N E R G Y...

To make me strong, to help me grow,
I eat to: ready, steady ... GO!
And what about the extra goo?
Well that comes out, of course, in POO!

Food gives us the energy we
need to play, learn, grow and repair.
What's your favourite food?

11

I hope you have finished, as soon we will see
The food that an ogre would like for **his** tea...

Bogies in jelly spread thickly on bread,
Or runny-nose smoothies with dribble instead?

Toenail tortillas and fingernail chips,
Used to scoop up a selection of dips...

Snot with a sprinkle of sneeze on the side,
Or sleepy-dust bits either scrambled or fried?

12

Sweaty foot cheese from a sock never washed,
Cooked in a stew until chewy and squashed...

Pasta shaped out of the wax from your ears,
Boiled in a pan full of saltwater tears?

"Oh," says the Ogre,
"I don't mean to boast
But I'd much rather guzzle...
A small child on toast!"

Did you manage to read this ogre tongue twister without saying YUCK?

Why do our bodies produce all of this gunk? Turn the page to find out...

What are tears for?

What is spit for?

What is sleepy-dust for?

What is sweat for?

What is earwax for?

What are bogies for?

14

Tears are for crying, whatever your size,
Tears are the water that washes your eyes.

Slurping and licking and squishing and smoothing,
Mixing and chewing to keep the food moving.

The crust that collects in your eyes every night
Is just dust, oil and tears and it keeps your eyes bright.

Turn up the heat and your body will sweat,
Cooling you down just by making you wet!

Sticky and yellow, this wax is protection
Made just for your ears – it's to fight off infection.

Filtering, sneezing – oh, what a surprise –
Snot forms a pick-able crust when it dries.

The bogies, spit, sweat, tears and other bits are all there to protect the body and help it run smoothly. It's not GROSS – it's GREAT!

I hear the next ride as it stops with a 'thud!'
Now we are going to visit some ... BLOOD!

Whooshing and flowing, first slower, then faster,
Better not fall or you might need a plaster!

Blood full of good stuff that runs through our veins,
Red runny blood from our toes to our brains...

Hard-working blood for delivering, sending,
Collecting and carrying, healing and mending.

How many things does the blood have to give?
Blood contains everything needed to live!

Thicker than water and thinner than mud,
This is the liquid we all know as blood.

Deep in our chest is the very best part,
That handsome, magnificent organ: the HEART.

The heart is a muscle for pushing and pumping and
While we're alive it will never stop thumping...

Slow beats for thinking, relaxing and sleeping,
Fast beats when frightened or running and leaping!

Duh-duh, duh-duh...
and a thumpety-thud...

...this is the sound as the heart pumps the blood.

Blood carries food and oxygen to all the organs around the body. Blood also repairs and takes away carbon dioxide and other waste.

Where are we going? I see at a glance...
We have arrived at a skeleton dance.

A skull and two cross bones, a black and white flag,
I spy a pirate, but where is his swag?

I hear the music and there is the band,
Hurry up lazybones – come take my hand!

Shaking our bones to the musical beat,
Dance to your favourite tunes then repeat.

Bones can be curvy or stretch in a line,
33 bones in my back make a spine.

Bones in my fingers and bones in my toes,
Bones in my legs – but no bones in my nose...

Bones are connected like words in a song,
Bones hold us up – help us walk – they are strong.

Rattle your bones, come and dance 'til you drop,
Join in the fun at the skeleton bop!

Some bones support our body and some protect our organs and insides. Spread your fingers wide – can you see the bones in your hands?

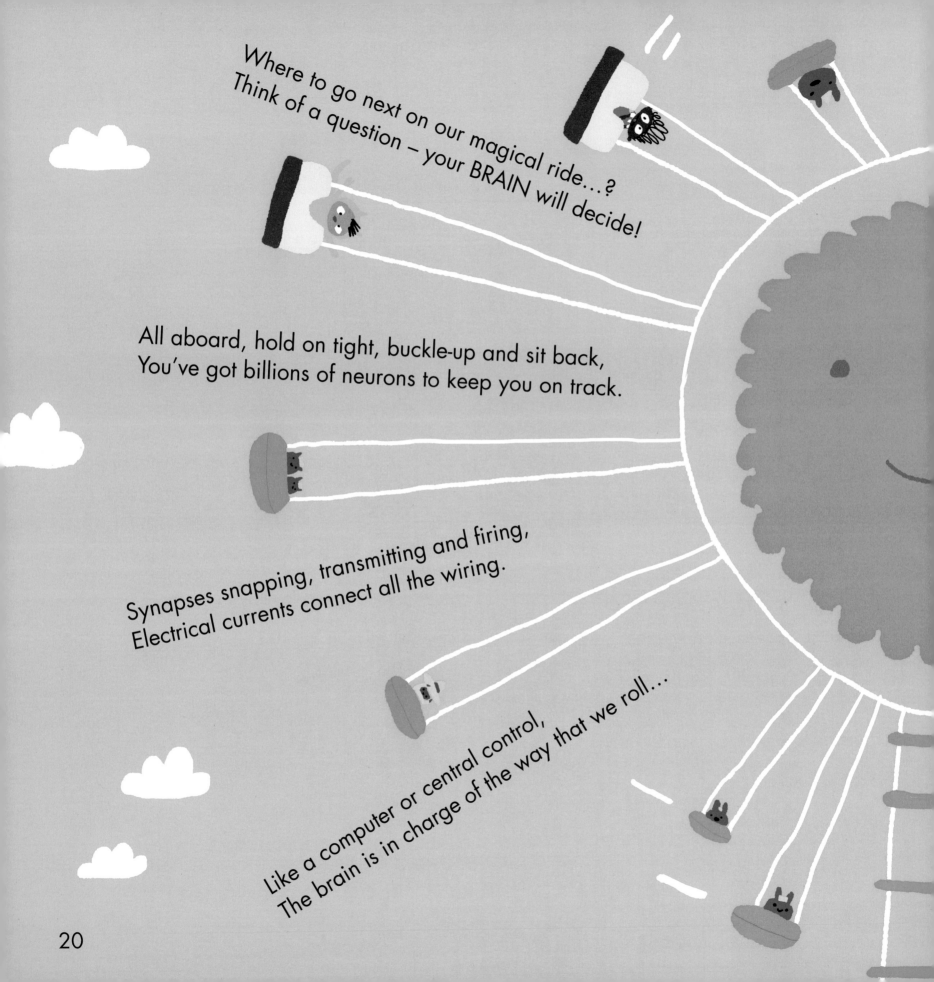

Where to go next on our magical ride...?
Think of a question – your BRAIN will decide!

All aboard, hold on tight, buckle-up and sit back,
You've got billions of neurons to keep you on track.

Synapses snapping, transmitting and firing,
Electrical currents connect all the wiring.

Like a computer or central control,
The brain is in charge of the way that we roll...

Thinking, remembering, making things clear,
The brain is the best when you need an idea.

Learning and solving again and again,
You have a beautiful, brilliant brain!

Come and explore and I think you will find
That the power of YOU is contained in your MIND...

The brain is a large, wrinkly organ in your head that is in charge of making things happen. It tells the lungs to keep breathing, controls digestion and lets the heart know how fast to beat. The brain is the centre of learning and balancing, dreaming and having BIG and small ideas.

Your brain commands all the other parts of the body, because ... your brain is BOSS!

21

Now it's time to swim the oceans
Of those things we call: EMOTIONS…

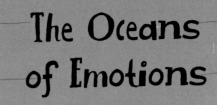

The Oceans of Emotions

Feeling good, feeling bad, often happy, sometimes sad…

Feeling stupid, feeling bright, feeling wrong but I'm all right!

Feeling giggly, now I'm wired, feeling cross then very tired…

Feeling little, growing tall … now I'm big and next I'm small!

Feeling full, feeling sick, starting slow then going quick...

Feeling sweet, or sometimes sour, feeling weak – now feel my POWER!

Sometimes feeling not a lot. Sometimes feeling not sure what...

What a lot of things to feel – feelings mean we know it's REAL!

Our feelings and emotions are what make us human. There are so many of them! What makes you HAPPY? What makes you SAD? How many feelings can you count?

Ding!

23

Take a deep breath – we are lifting so high!
Up and away as we float through the sky...

So how do lungs work?
Well I have little doubt
That at first they breathe in,
and then they breathe out.

Have you noticed how BREATHING speeds up when you run?
Or do anything active, exciting or fun...

Lungs can expand like a giant balloon...
All that air comes in handy for ... playing a tune!

And even when breathing slows down as you rest,
Those two lungs keep on working away in your chest!

Oxygen gas is what keeps us alive,
So it's breathing fresh air that will help us to thrive.

Lungs take all the oxygen – send out the waste
From invisible air you can't touch nor can taste.

And guess what? All the stuff that us humans don't need
Is the gas that for plants is the best kind of feed!

Breathing is automatic.
All you need is a pair of LUNGS
and some air. We breathe in OXYGEN
gas and breathe out CARBON DIOXIDE
gas (it's the waste).

How exhausting! Time to float aboard a noisy body boat.

Hum and whistle, click and squeak, laugh and giggle, sing and speak.

Breathe in, breathe out, quiet whisper, LOUD SHOUT!

Wheeze and croak, cough and splutter, tittle, tattle, mumble, mutter.

First a tickle, then a sneeze, pass a tissue quickly please!

Hubble, bubble, glug and rumble, hungry tummy – what a grumble!

Chew and swallow, crunch and munch – noises when you eat your lunch.

Sip your drink, but if you slurp, catching air will make you BURP!

All the gas that stops and starts, out it comes in bottom farts!

Often funny, quite bizarre, what a noisy lot we are...

Our bodies make so many different sounds: from digesting food gurgles, coughs and sneezes to breathing and burping. How many body noises can YOU make?

27

We're by the sea, beside the fair. Now can you spot the 'senses' here?

I see the sea splash on the beach,
I spy the boat just out of reach.
I taste the salt and breathe the air,
I jump the waves without a care.

And from the corner of my eye,
I spot a seagull in the sky.
I hear a squawk and then a screech,
And watch it circling round the beach.

I taste the ice cream on my tongue
That's melting in the warming sun.
I feel the tickle on my skin
As ice cream trickles down my chin.

I climb the rocks, I touch the top
I shudder as I spy the drop –
I turn towards the sea once more
And watch the waves break on the shore.

I build a castle in the sand
And let the grains run through my hand...
I pick up pebbles smooth and round,
And search for treasures lost and found.

And as I look for distant ships,
I smell my supper: fish and chips!
I love it here beside the sea
I feel alive. I feel I'm ME!

SENSES are how we experience the world around us. There are five main senses – did you spot them all here? Sight, smell, hearing, touch and taste.

29

I am riding along in a carriage…
Like a king or a queen from the past.
I'm beginning to doze as my eyes start to close,
I am falling, first slowly then fast…

And I run like a fox in the moonlight
Or a cat jumping over a wall.

I am silent and wait by the side of the gate
In the shadows … I'm not there at all.

In a space on the edge of the ocean,
Where the waves touch the tip of the shore,
There are fishes that dance and I know at a glance
It's a place I would love to explore!

30

With a leap I am high over forests,
And I fly through the stars to the moon!
From the darkness ahead, I look back to my bed
And decide to return to it soon...

So I fall from the sky, past a mountain
Where the flowers all sing with a yawn:
"Go to sleep, sleepyhead!" as I tumble to bed...

And I dream about ice cream 'til dawn...

31

GLOSSARY

CARBON DIOXIDE (CO2) The gas you breathe out

DIGESTING The process of breaking down food in the tummy (stomach) and intestines into smaller parts so it can be used by your body for energy

DYNAMITE An explosive

EMOTIONS Strong feelings that can change according to what's happening around us

INFECTION When a germ gets into your body and causes illness

LARGE INTESTINE The last part of the digesting process where poo is made

NEURONS A special nerve cell that can send messages to your brain and body

ORGAN Part of the body that has a special job, for example, the heart pumps blood around your body

OXYGEN The gas you breathe in

POO The solid waste that is left over after digesting food

REPAIR To fix something that is damaged

SPINE A row of bones running down your back

SYNAPSE The tiny gap between neurons which messages travel across

WASTE Something that is not needed

NOTES FOR PARENTS, CARERS AND TEACHERS

This book explores the human body in a fun and accessible way, and can be used with children to develop their own self-confidence and self-awareness. It is designed to be shared with children on many different levels, from encouraging them to ask questions about their own physical development, to prompting them to jump up and dance around! You can also use the book to lead further investigation into how our bodies work, and to anchor language teaching through physical movement.

Franklin Watts
First published in
Great Britain in 2017 by
The Watts Publishing Group

Text © Gabby Dawnay 2017
Illustrations © Alex Barrow 2017

All rights reserved.

Executive editor: Adrian Cole
Design manager: Peter Scoulding
Consultant: Jackie Hamley

With special thanks to children's arts and science magazine OKIDO, GD and AB

ISBN: 978 1 4451 5202 8

Printed in China

Franklin Watts
An imprint of
Hachette Children's Group
Part of The Watts Publishing Group
Carmelite House
50 Victoria Embankment
London EC4Y 0DZ

An Hachette UK Company
www.hachette.co.uk

www.franklinwatts.co.uk